JUDE THE OBSCURE

NOTES

including
- *Hardy's Life and Career*
- *Brief Synopsis*
- *List of Characters*
- *Chapter Summaries and Commentaries*
- *Analyses of Main Characters*
- *Critical Analysis of the Novel*
- *Review Questions and Theme Topics*
- *Selected Bibliography*

by
Frank H. Thompson, Jr., M.A.
University of Nebraska

INCORPORATED

LINCOLN, NEBRASKA 68501

Editor

Gary Carey, M.A.
University of Colorado

Consulting Editor

James L. Roberts, Ph.D.
Department of English
University of Nebraska

4-24-00   Moonbeam Pub./5.00

ISBN 0-8220-0690-1
© Copyright 1966
by
Cliffs Notes, Inc.
All Rights Reserved
Printed in U.S.A.

1999 Printing

Cliffs Notes, Inc.   Lincoln, Nebraska

CONTENTS

Jude the Obscure

HARDY'S LIFE AND CAREER

Born on June 2, 1840, in Upper Bockhampton, not far from Dorchester, in Dorsetshire, Thomas Hardy was the son of Thomas Hardy, a master mason or building contractor, and Jemima Hand, a woman of some literary interests. Hardy's formal education consisted of only some eight years in local schools, but by the end of this period he had on his own read a good deal in English, French, and Latin, just as later in London he made his own rather careful study of painting and English poetry. He was also interested in music and learned to play the violin. At the age of sixteen he was apprenticed to an architect in Dorchester and remained in that profession, later in London and then again in Dorchester, for almost twenty years.

He began to write poetry during this time, but none of it was published. His first novel, *The Poor Man and the Lady*, written in 1867-68, was never published, and the manuscript did not survive except insofar as Hardy used parts of it in other books. His first published novel was *Desperate Remedies* in 1871; the first novel which came out in serial form before publication as a book, an arrangement he was to follow for the rest of his novels, was *A Pair of Blue Eyes* in 1873; his real fame as a novelist, along with sufficient income to enable him to abandon architecture for good, came with *Far from the Madding Crowd* in 1874. On September 17, 1874, Hardy married Emma Lavinia Gifford.

From this time on Hardy devoted his full time to writing, continuing to publish novels regularly until his last in 1895, *Jude the Obscure*. Among these are some of the best of his so-called Wessex novels (Hardy was, incidentally, the first to refer to Dorset as Wessex): *The Return of the Native*, 1878; *The Mayor of Casterbridge*, 1886; *The Woodlanders*, 1887; *Tess of the D'Urbervilles*, 1891; in addition to *Jude*. To this list of best should be added the earlier *Far from the Madding Crowd*. In writing most of his novels,

Hardy meticulously worked out the details of time and geography he wanted to use; almost every novel is, therefore, located in a carefully mapped out area of Wessex and covers a specified period of time. *Jude the Obscure*, for example, covers the period 1855-74 and is set principally in Fawley, Oxford, and Salisbury (called in the novel Marygreen, Christminster, and Melchester). *Tess* sold more rapidly than any of his other novels, and *Jude* was probably more vehemently denounced. During this period of time Hardy also published his first poems as well as short stories. On June 29, 1885 he moved into a house he had built in Dorchester and lived there for the rest of his life.

On November 27, 1912, Mrs. Hardy died, a woman with whom he had become increasingly incompatible; and on February 10 1914, he married Florence Emily Dugdale, a woman whom he had referred to for several years previously as his assistant and who was about forty years younger than he. After the appearance of *Jude* Hardy devoted his attention entirely to poetry and drama, publishing a number of books of poems, including one which he prepared just before his death. He also wrote and published an epic drama on the Napoleonic era, *The Dynasts*, which appeared in three parts with a total of nineteen acts. He was given a number of honors, including an honorary degree from Oxford, which he had criticized so severely in *Jude*. The success of *Tess* had made possible a good income from his writing for the rest of his life, and when he died he left an estate of nearly half a million dollars. He died on January 11 1928, and a few days later was buried in Westminster Abbey.

BRIEF SYNOPSIS

Jude Fawley, an eleven-year-old boy, wants to follow the example of his teacher Mr. Phillotson, who leaves Marygreen for Christminster to take a university degree and to be ordained. Jude is being raised by his great-aunt, whom he helps in her bakery. He studies very hard on his own to prepare for the move, and to provide a means by which he can support himself at the university, he learns the trade of ecclesiastical stonework. He meets, desires, and marries Arabella Donn, who deceives him into marriage by making him think he has got her pregnant. They do not get along at all, and eventually Arabella leaves him to go with her family to Australia.

Though delayed, Jude does get to Christminster, partly because of his aspirations but also partly because of the presence there of his cousin Sue Bridehead. He meets and falls in love with her, though the fact of his being married causes him to feel guilty. Sue will not return his love, and when he realizes that Phillotson, under whom she is now teaching, is interested in Sue, Jude is in despair. This plus the fact that he has made no headway on getting into the university and realizes he never will causes him to give up that part of his dream and leave Christminster.

At Melchester he intends to pursue theological study and eventually enter the church at a lower level. Sue is there at a training college and is to marry Phillotson when she finishes, but she flees the school when punished for staying out all night with Jude. Jude is puzzled by Sue because her ideas are different from his and she will not return the feeling he has for her.

Shortly after he tells her he is married, she announces her marriage to Phillotson and asks Jude to give her away. He sees Arabella again, who is back from abroad, spends the night with her, and learns that she married in Australia. When he next encounters Sue, she tells him perhaps she shouldn't have married, and Jude vows to go on seeing her in spite of his aim to discipline himself to get into the church.

When Jude's aunt dies, Sue comes to Marygreen for the funeral, and there she admits to him she is unhappy and can't give herself to Phillotson. The kiss Jude and Sue exchange when she leaves for Shaston causes him to think he has reached the point where he is no longer fit for the church; therefore, he burns his theological books and will profess nothing.

Sue asks Phillotson to let her live apart from him, preferably with Jude, but he only allows her to live apart in the house until an instance of her repugnance to him causes him to decide to let her go. Sue goes to Jude and they travel to Aldbrickham, but she will

not yet allow intimacy. Phillotson is dismissed from his job at
Shaston when Sue never returns, and after seeing her later and not
being able to get her back he decides to divorce her to give her
complete freedom.

After living together a year at Aldbrickham Jude and Sue have
still not consummated their relationship, and though they repeat
edly plan to be married they never go through with it. Only when
Arabella appears and seems to threaten her hold on Jude does Sue
allow intimacy. Arabella marries Cartlett, her Australian husband
again and sends to Jude her and Jude's son, Little Father Time.

When opinion turns against Jude and Sue and he loses a job
because of their reputation, they decide to leave Aldbrickham, and
they live in many places as Jude works where he can find employ
ment in anything other than ecclesiastical work, which he decides
to give up. They now have two children of their own and another on
the way. Having seen Sue in Kennetbridge, Arabella, whose hus
band has died, revives her interest in Jude, and when she encoun
ters Phillotson, who is now in Marygreen, she tells him he was
wrong to let Sue go. Jude, now ill and not working regularly, wants
to return to Christminster.

They do return to Christminster, arriving on a holiday, and
Jude is upset by his return to the city that has meant so much to
him and gives a speech to a street crowd in an attempt to explain
what his life has meant. Despairing talk by Sue triggers off a reac
tion in Little Father Time, and he hangs the other two children and
himself. And the child Sue is carrying is born dead. Jude and Sue
have reached the point where their views of life have about re
versed, Jude becoming secular and Sue religious; and when Phillot
son writes to ask Sue to come back to him, she agrees, thinking
of it as a penance.

Sue returns to Phillotson at Marygreen and marries him again
though she still finds him repugnant. Arabella comes to Jude, and
by persistent scheming she gets him to marry her once more. They
get along about as before, and though ill Jude goes to see Sue and
they declare their love for each other. As a further penance, Sue

hen gives herself to Phillotson. Jude learns of this, and on the
holiday the following year, while Arabella is out enjoying the
festivities, Jude dies. Only Arabella and Mrs. Edlin are present
to stand watch by his coffin.

LIST OF CHARACTERS

Jude Fawley

A young man of obscure origins who aspires to a university
education and a place in the church and who learns the trade of
ecclesiastical stonework to help him realize his goals.

Sue Bridehead

Jude's cousin, an intelligent, unconventional young woman
whom Jude loves and lives with but who is twice married to Phillotson.

Arabella Donn

A sensually attractive young woman whom Jude marries twice
and who in between is married to Cartlett.

Richard Phillotson

Jude's former teacher who has the same aspirations as his pupil.

Little Father Time (Jude)

The son of Jude and Arabella.

Drusilla Fawley

Jude's great-aunt, who raises Jude.

Physician Vilbert

A quack doctor of local reputation.

Mrs. Edlin

A widow who looks after Drusilla Fawley before she dies and
who is a friend to Jude and Sue.

Mr. Donn
Arabella's father, a pig farmer and later owner of a pork shop.

Anny
A girl friend of Arabella's.

Cartlett
Arabella's "Australian husband."

George Gillingham
A teacher friend of Phillotson's.

Tinker Taylor
A "decayed church-ironmonger" and drinking companion of Jude's.

Chapter Summaries and Commentaries

PART FIRST

CHAPTERS 1-2

Summary

The schoolmaster, Mr. Phillotson, is preparing to leave the village of Marygreen in Wessex. He is bound for Christminster, where he intends to take a university degree and then be ordained. He is helped in his preparation by Jude Fawley, an eleven-year-old boy who has been his student and who admires him. Phillotson has given the boy a book as a farewell gift, and the schoolmaster tells Jude to look him up if he ever comes to Christminster. After Phillotson leaves, Jude stands thinking of the schoolmaster at the old well, to which he has come originally to draw water for his great-aunt and which is one of few old parts of the village still remaining, the rest having been replaced by more modern structures, most notably the church.

Returning to the house with water from the well, Jude hears his great-aunt, Drusilla Fawley, who runs a bakery in the house, n conversation with some friends. When he enters the room, his aunt explains to her friends the circumstances of Jude's life that brought him into her care a year before. She describes him as bookish, like his cousin Sue, and tells him that he should never marry, since the Fawleys are unlucky in matrimony. Jude goes off to his job in Farmer Troutham's cornfields, where he is supposed to scare off the rooks with a noisemaker. Depressed by the ugliness of the fields and sympathetic with the birds' hunger, he soon gives up his noisemaking and happily watches the birds eat. He is caught by Troutham, reprimanded, and punished for deserting his duties, and dismissed from his job. His aunt is annoyed by his now having nothing to occupy him and wonders aloud why he didn't go off with the schoolteacher to Christminster. Jude asks her about this city but is told he'll never be able to have anything to do with it. Jude leaves, reflecting on the difficulties of growing up and the incomprehensibility of life. He decides to see Christminster and starts off, his direction necessarily taking him back through Farmer Troutham's fields.

Commentary

The use of a series of short scenes to develop the plot is typical of Hardy's narrative technique and is exemplified in the opening chapters. The last of these four or five scenes, in fact, is continued into Chapter 3; this too occurs several times in the novel. There are very few scenes which could be called long; the longest, perhaps, occurs when Sue comes to Jude's lodgings after fleeing from the training school in Melchester (Part Third, Chapters 3-5). In the present chapters, the plot moves smoothly from one scene to another, from Phillotson's loading his luggage to Jude's climbing up toward the ridge-track; in many cases, however, the transitions are abrupt and sometimes awkward.

These scenes serve to foreshadow a number of things that will occur later in the novel. Jude's admiration for Phillotson will shortly become a desire to emulate his teacher's ambitions and follow him to Christminster. Jude's inability to hurt any living creature, as Hardy explicitly points out, may cause him to suffer as he goes through life. Jude does not understand "nature's logic" and in reflecting on life thinks: "All around you there seemed to be something glaring, garish, rattling, and the noises and glares hit upon the little cell called your life, and shook it, and warped it." This too is full of suggestion as to what Jude's life will show.

The setting for this novel is, of course, Hardy's Wessex, which he invented and used in a series of novels. Several aspects of that "landscape" are of interest here. Marygreen, it is said, is changing: few of the old structures are still in existence; an outstanding example of the new is the church, which is of "modern Gothic design." The well at which Jude stands is one of few old things left in the village.

Some of the characters in the novel are used as a part of this local landscape and reflect its history and customs. Aunt Drusilla is one of these, with her talk about Jude's family and her foreboding comment that the Fawleys are luckless in marriage, both Jude and his cousin Sue having been victims of that bad luck.

Above all, what is strongly suggested in these opening scenes is the coming of the new and the dying out of the old, the effects of which go to form the theme of the novel. It is the spirit of the modern that makes itself felt in this place and on these characters. Its effects will be widespread, as suggested here, ranging all the way from Jude's desire to better himself to large questions about the nature of the universe and the power that governs it.

CHAPTERS 3-4

Summary

At first when Jude reaches a high point outside of town, the "ridge-track," he cannot see Christminster; nor can he see it from the roof of a barn nearby, locally called the Brown House. He waits patiently, prays for the visibility to improve, and finally just before sunset does see light reflected from buildings in the city. Frequently thereafter he comes to this high place to look, occasionally at night. On one such occasion he encounters a man driving a wagon who talks to him about Christminster, describing it as a place of learning, religion, and beautiful music. After listening to the carter's account, all secondhand, Jude decides this is the place that may satisfy his need for a foundation. He calls Christminster "a city of light."

Walking home after the occasion of his conversation with the carter, Jude encounters Physician Vilbert, a quack doctor of local reputation. After seeking confirmation of his exalted view of Christminster from the man, Jude says he wants to learn Latin and Greek and offers to advertise Vilbert's pills if the physician will get grammars of the two languages for him. The man agrees, and Jude works hard for two weeks to get orders for him. When they meet again as arranged, Jude has orders for him, the physician has forgotten the books, and the boy realizes the man has no interest in his aspirations. When Phillotson sends for the piano he has left behind, stored with Jude's aunt, Jude encloses in the packing case a request for the grammars. When they eventually arrive, Jude discovers to his dismay that there is no rule or secret by which the words of his own language can be changed into those of Latin or Greek. Appalled by the labor of learning a language word by word and amazed at what prodigious intellects the learned men of Christminster must have, Jude throws the books aside and wishes he had never seen a book and had never been born.

Commentary

Hardy uses a series of major and minor symbols to help convey the meaning of his novel. Certainly one of the major ones is Christminster. In these chapters Jude is to be seen making Christminster into a symbol of all that is good and meaningful in his life. He looks at it from a distance both in the daytime and at night. He wonders where in the lights of the city Phillotson may be. He inquires of everyone he meets about life in that place: workmen, a carter, a quack doctor. From the common talk about it that they repeat to him he forms an idea of it as a "city of light." He even puts himself to the task of learning Latin and Greek on his own in order to be accepted there, and the grammars he finally gets come from a lucky inhabitant of that place, Phillotson.

Considering his age, Jude is likely to have fixed the meaning of Christminster to him forever in his mind. And that meaning, in turn, will affect his own life at every step, as it will affect the lives of others who come into contact with him.

14

CHAPTER 5

Summary

During the next few years Jude tries to educate himself b
reading Latin and some Greek with the use of a dictionary. Thi
study takes place as he drives the bakery wagon for his aunt's ex
panding business, paying more attention to his reading than to wher
he is going or with whom he is supposed to do business. One da
when he is sixteen he stops near the Brown House, kneels by th
side of the road, and reads aloud a poem he has been reading i
honor of the then setting sun and rising moon. This pagan impuls
causes Jude to wonder if he as a future minister hasn't spent to
much time on secular works. He then takes up the study of the Nev
Testament in Greek and eventually theological works.

In order to make possible his future move to Christminster
Jude decides he must have a trade to support himself. He choose
ecclesiastical stonework because of his interest in medieval art an
also because of the fact that his cousin Sue's father had been a
ecclesiastical metalworker. Apprenticing himself in the nearby tow
of Alfredston, he begins to learn his trade. At the age of ninetee
Jude is living in the town during the week and returning to Mary
green every Saturday evening.

Commentary

This is an instance of a transition chapter. Its purpose is to spa
the time from Jude's decision to go to Christminster to that point a
which he has learned as much as he can on his own but is not quit
ready financially. Some six or seven years pass, during which, a
shown in summary, he studies constantly on his own and begins t
learn a trade in order to support himself. There is only one brie
scene, but it is presented descriptively rather than dramatically

Jude's choice of occupation is one of many ironies in the nove
It is established in the very first chapter that even in a small villag
like Marygreen the old style of church is being replaced. His deliber
ate choice of ecclesiastical stonework in medieval Gothic style
therefore, will limit his opportunity to work, though of course h
doesn't realize it. The fact that he chooses this craft partly becaus
he likes medieval art and culture will be later, when his views change
one of the reasons for which he will give up working on churches

CHAPTERS 6-8

Summary

One weekend as he walks home from Alfredston, Jude makes an accounting of what he has accomplished to the age of nineteen. He believes he has some fluency in Latin and Greek, both Homeric and Biblical; he has studied some mathematics, theology, and history. What he does not yet know he will learn at Christminster, where books and instruction await him. As soon as he saves more money he will be off. He dreams of getting his D.D. and becoming a bishop or perhaps an archdeacon. He is brought back to reality by being hit on the ear by something, and he realizes that on the other side of the hedge is a pig farm and he hears girls' voices. After a bantering conversation as to who threw the pig's offal at him, Jude asks one of the three girls if she wants to meet him. They do meet on a plank bridge across the stream alongside which the girls have been working; the girl is Arabella Donn. Jude finds her attractive, aware of girls as such for the first time. Arabella easily maneuvers Jude into calling on her the next day, a Sunday. When he walks off again, his single-minded concentration on getting to Christminster fades before the onrush of new emotions.

On Sunday afternoon, which he has set aside to read in his new Greek Testament, Jude easily convinces himself to keep his date with Arabella. In going for a walk they pass the Brown House, from which eminence Jude has often looked out at Christminster. Walking farther than intended, they stop at an inn for tea, sitting in a room on the wall of which is a picture of Samson and Delilah. Unable to get tea, they settle for beer, and Jude is surprised at Arabella's knowledge of its ingredients. They then walk to Arabella's house in the dark, several times stopping to kiss, Jude finally holding her close as they walk. As he walks home later, Jude is impatient of the fact that he must wait a whole week to see her again. Next day, Arabella declares to her two girl friends she wants to marry Jude, and they tease her because she says she doesn't know how to make sure she gets him. One of them whispers to her, and she obviously has told Arabella to let Jude get her pregnant.

Passing the Donn farm one weekend on his way home from Alfredston, Jude encounters Arabella chasing some newly acquired pigs which have got out of the sty. Giving up the chase of the last one, they lie down on a hilltop, and when Arabella can't get Jude to caress her as she wishes she pretends to be affronted and goes off home. When the next day, Sunday, Arabella hears talk of Jude's going to Christminster, she decides to get him to make love to her, in short, to carry out the plan suggested by her girl friends. She arranges to get her parents out of the house that evening, and when she and Jude are alone in the house she teases him with a cochin's egg she is carrying in her bosom to hatch, an old custom, she says. Exciting Jude by removing it and replacing it several times, Arabella gets him to pursue her. She disappears upstairs and Jude follows her. Obviously they make love.

Commentary

Now that Jude thinks he is about ready for Christminster, it is dramatically as well as thematically the time to introduce the first of a series of conflicts that by the end of the novel changes his life and his hopes radically. It is appropriate that the first should be occasioned by a woman.

At the beginning of the scene in Chapter 6 Jude is walking home from work, mentally adding up his accomplishments of the past few years, estimating how close he is to Christminster and what rewards it will bring. At the end of the scene he realizes he is putting aside his ambitions but can think only of the "fresh and wild pleasure" which Arabella promises. In between he is introduced to sex. Hardy makes it clear that Arabella is attractive but not unusually beautiful, that she deliberately attracts his attention, and that when they meet she flirts with him. In short, she does what any other girl might do. Her effect on Jude comes from an awakening in him over which, it is said, he has no control.

This coming to awareness of sex conflicts, of course, with the aspirations Christminster represents; but it is also the introduction into his life of a desire or need which he will try always to satisfy, with consequent effects on other areas of his life.

The use of the minor symbol of Samson and Delilah, appearing in this section first and then several times later in the novel, is appropriate to the idea Hardy is trying to convey by introducing Arabella into Jude's life. Here the symbol appears in the form of a picture on the wall of an inn; elsewhere, it appears in other forms, for instance, in a description of Jude as Arabella looks at him.

CHAPTER 9

Summary

Two months later, Arabella tells Jude she is pregnant, and though he has said it is time for him to leave for Christminster he promises to marry her, speaking of his aspirations as impossible dreams. They marry and go to live in a cottage alongside the road between the Brown House and Marygreen. Jude quickly discovers several things about his wife: that she wears false hair, that she was once a barmaid, that the dimples in her cheeks are artificially produced. After admitting to one of her friends that she isn't pregnant at all, Arabella is apprehensive about telling Jude. When she does, he sees how unnecessary the marriage is; Arabella is complacent in her legal status. He wonders to himself about the justice of a society that causes an individual to have to forego his highest aspirations.

Commentary

When Jude finds out that Arabella is not pregnant, some very disturbing thoughts pass through his mind: "He was inclined to inquire what he had done, or she lost, for that matter, that he deserved to be caught in a gin which would cripple him, if not her also, for the rest of a lifetime?" Later, of course, he discovers that she deliberately enticed him to make love to her so that she could claim to be pregnant. Hardy already has had Jude as a boy wonder what it is that noisily seems to warp one's life.

What comes out here, as elsewhere, is part of Hardy's theme in the novel: Jude's beliefs, conventionally Christian as they are, cannot account for what is happening to him. Something blind or malign is operating to undermine his dream. In short, the old explanations do not seem to account for life. By the end of the novel Jude will be shown in a self-admitted "chaos of principles." Here, he is just becoming aware of the disparity between what he has been taught to believe and what the circumstances of his life confront him with.

CHAPTERS 10-11

Summary

When the pig killer doesn't come to kill the pig Jude and Arabella have been fattening, Jude is forced to do the job. He wants to kill it quickly so as to be merciful, but Arabella insists it should

18

slowly bleed to death so that the meat will be better. Jude sticks the pig deeply and it bleeds quickly, much to Arabella's disgust and anger. Coming home from work that day, he overhears Arabella's girl friend tell another girl she put Arabella up to tricking Jude. When he confronts Arabella with this, she makes light of it, saying many girls work the same deception. But Jude insists she was wrong to so trap him into a marriage satisfactory to neither of them.

When the next morning, a Sunday, in the course of her work with the pig's fat Arabella tosses some of Jude's books aside, he gets angry at her. She leaves the house and, disheveled, walks up and down the road in front, lamenting her ill-treatment and accusing Jude of being like his father and his father's sister in their relationship to their spouses. When Jude goes to his aunt to ask her about this, she tells him his parents couldn't get along and separated, his mother later drowning herself. His father's sister couldn't get along with her husband and eventually left him, taking her daughter Sue with her.

In despair Jude walks out onto the ice of a pond as if to drown himself, but the ice doesn't break. He decides to do something more suitable to his degraded state and goes to get drunk. Coming home later, he discovers Arabella has gone, leaving him a note that she will not return. In a few days she writes to say she wants no more of him and she is going with her family to Australia. Jude replies that he has no objection and sends her money as well as his household goods for her to include in the auction the family is going to have.

Later, in a secondhand store he discovers among the goods from the sale that the dealer has bought a photograph he gave Arabella. This puts an end to whatever feeling he may yet have for her. On a stroll one evening he comes to the place on the ridge-track from which he has so often looked for Christminster and realizes that though much has happened he has still not achieved his ambitions. These ambitions are reawakened by his seeing on the back of a milestone nearby an inscription he carved to symbolize his goal in life. He decides to go to Christminster as soon as his apprenticeship has ended.

Commentary

Several aspects of the setting are made use of in these chapters. The Brown House on the ridge-track was important earlier as marking the spot from which Jude first looked out at Christminster. Now, is revealed that he inscribed a symbol of his aspirations on the back of a nearby milestone. Jude also learns that his parents separated in this very same location, and his aunt hints too that a gallows which once stood here is somehow connected with the history of the family (much later in the novel, Jude hears this tale from Mrs. Edlin).

It is said that Arabella's deception of Jude is a common practice in the locality if a girl wants to make sure she gets the man she chooses to marry her. Above all, there is the killing of the pig, a commonplace practice certainly but one which is used here to reveal important differences between Jude and Arabella. To her the killing of the pig is an ordinary action to be done in a businesslike way. To Jude it is an occasion for scruples. As a person who is said to be unable to hurt any living thing, he is forced into being the one who kills the pig. He doesn't want to do it and tries to kill it quickly, contrary to the best local practice. His desire not to let the pig suffer is reflected later in the novel when he mercifully puts an end to a rabbit caught in a trap. And he himself, near the end of his life, wishes someone would dispatch him as he killed the pig.

The vivid details of this last scene, incidentally, were found disgusting by many of Hardy's contemporary readers, the contention being, apparently, that realism can be carried too far.

PART SECOND

CHAPTER 1

Summary

Three years later, his apprenticeship ended, Jude is on his way to Christminster. Not only have his old aspirations caused him to come; but he has seen a photograph of his cousin Sue Bridehead and has been told by his aunt that the girl lives in the city. He arrives at sunset, finds himself lodgings in an inexpensive suburb nicknamed Beersheba, and goes to look over the city. He has read and thought so much about it that as he wanders among the ancient colleges he seems to encounter the ghosts of the famous men associated with them. Back in his lodgings, before he falls asleep he seems to hear these men speak to him in words that he has read.

Commentary

For Jude Christminster is as much a dream when he is actually there as when he viewed it from the ridge-track outside Marygreen. It is significant that his first contact with the place is at night, a time when it is easier for him to make the physical facts conform to his idea. He studies the buildings of the colleges with great care and soon seems to encounter the ghosts of the great men of the past who were associated with Christminster. Even when he returns to his lodgings, their words fill his head before he goes to sleep.

Jude has finally got to Christminster, but it is a Christminster of his imagination, one that very likely never existed at all.

CHAPTERS 2-3

Summary

Jude's first concern is a job, though his working is to be done only as a way of supporting himself until he can enter the university. He goes to apply to a stonemason recommended by his employer in Alfredston. While there, he notices that the workmen are doing only copying and patching, not realizing that medieval building is coming to an end. He decides, while waiting to hear about the job, not to look up either Sue or Phillotson as yet. Now actually in Christminster he sees how really far away he is from realizing his dream, but he takes the job when offered and sets to work studying late into the night, as before not knowing what the best way is to go about it. By means of word from his aunt he comes upon Sue working in an ecclesiastical warehouse; though he is struck by her appearance and the work she is doing he doesn't speak to her. Nor does he when he sees her on the street. He decides he must think of Sue only as a relative for several reasons: he is married; it is no good for cousins to fall in love; and the family's bad luck in marriage would be even worse with a blood relative.

Though Jude sees Sue at a church service, at the moment feeling repentant of his sensual interest in Arabella, he does not reveal himself to her because he isn't sure of his motives for wanting to know her. Earlier than this incident, while on an afternoon's holiday Sue has bought plaster reproductions of statues of Venus and Apollo. Once home with them—she lives where she works—she doesn't know how to conceal them from the very pious woman who is both her employer and landlady. When the lady sees them wrapped in a corner of her room, Sue refers to them as saints. Alone in her room later, she places the figures on a chest of drawers in front of a print of a crucifixion, from time to time looking up at them from her copy of Gibbon. In another part of the city Jude is earnestly reading his Greek Testament.

Commentary

Here Hardy uses contrasting scenes to show the difference between Jude's impression of Sue and Sue as she actually is. Jude sees her first at work and remarks on what a "sweet, saintly, Christian business" she is in. On another occasion he sees her in church and concludes she is no doubt "steeped body and soul in church sentiment." But another scene shows her admiring and buying plaster reproductions of statues of Venus and Apollo and reading Edward Gibbon's *Decline and Fall of the Roman Empire*.

These scenes also help to indicate the differences in beliefs between Jude and Sue which go to make up part of the structure of the novel. That structure can be described as embodied in the reversals of belief in Jude and Sue, the changing marital relationships, and the slow, inevitable defeat of both. Jude's conventional beliefs are partly revealed in the authors he quotes from in the last chapter, as well as in his reverence for Christminster, the old university. Sue is shown to admire pagan statuary and to read the agnostic Gibbon, even as in a different part of the city Jude is poring over his New Testament in Greek.

These scenes also reveal part of the changes in Jude's emotional life. Arabella has left him; though he was attracted to her first of all as an object of sexual desire she proved to be incompatible in other ways. But the desire is aroused and always waiting to be satisfied. He is in love with Sue even before he meets her, though he is still married to Arabella. When he sees Sue he makes her into a saint, but beneath this veneer of interest he himself is aware that he wants her as a woman.

CHAPTER 4

Summary

Once more Jude has the opportunity to reveal himself to Sue but does not, still troubled by the legitimacy of his interest in her. He wants to pray to be delivered from temptation, but his every desire is precisely to be so tempted. Finally, it occurs that Sue looks him up at work, he is not there at the time, she sends him a note, he replies immediately when she says she may leave Christminster that he will meet her the same evening, and they do meet. Phillotson is mentioned in conversation, and Jude discovers he is still but a schoolmaster in Lumsdon just outside the city.

Jude and Sue walk out to call on Phillotson, and at first he does not remember Jude. Jude tells the older man that he is determined to follow his example, but Phillotson has given up his aspirations now except for the possibility of entering the church as a licentiate. Later as they walk back to the city, Sue explains why she plans to leave Christminster: her employer has seen her pagan statues and they have quarreled. Jude suggests she return to teaching, since Phillotson has said he needs help. Sue is interested, Jude convinces Phillotson to hire her if she is really interested, and Sue accepts the job.

Commentary

The scene in which Jude and Sue meet is used as a sharp contrast with that in which he and Arabella met. Sue does not scheme to meet him, she does not flirt with him, and during the whole time there is no element of sexual tension at all. As Jude himself sees, Sue acts more like a friend toward him than a woman. His feelings for her are more those of love than desire. Unlike Arabella, Sue is sensitive to place, does not want to meet on a "gloomy and inauspicious" spot. Arabella did not mind at all where they met, getting up from her work with the pigs' chitterlings to go to the plank bridge.

From the very beginning Jude is in no doubt about what Arabella represents to him. With Sue it is a different matter. From a distance she is a saint; when they meet he loves her more than ever; eventually, however, he will desire her too. Arabella represents no puzzle, but Sue will be an exasperating mystery to him for the rest of his life.

CHAPTER 5

Summary

Phillotson's interest in Sue quickly becomes more than that of a master in a new teacher. Though he is impressed by her ability as a teacher, he is also attracted to her as a person. On the occasion of their taking the pupils to Christminster to see a model of Jerusalem, Sue questions the authenticity of the reproduction and remarks, to Phillotson's surprise, that Jerusalem was certainly not first-rate by comparison with other ancient cities. They encounter Jude at the exhibition, and when Phillotson mentions Sue's criticizing the model Jude says he understands what she means.

A few days later a school inspector visits the school to observe Sue at work, and she is so upset that Phillotson has to look after her, assuring her with more than professional interest that she is the best teacher he's ever had. When Jude comes to visit them at Lumsdon, at their request, he observes their coming out of the vicarage together and Sue's not objecting to Phillotson's putting his arm around her waist. Jude returns to the city without calling on them, appalled at what he has been responsible for.

Commentary

Not only is the reader aware of the irony of Jude's introducing Sue to Phillotson, but Jude himself realizes it. He has gone out of his way to get Sue a job under Phillotson for entirely selfish reasons: he does not want her to leave Christminster, or the area close by. He wants to keep her near him. But when he goes to Lumsdon to visit her and sees Sue allow Phillotson to put his arm around her waist, he realizes that he has been the means by which the two are put into daily contact.

In the many ironies which occur in the novel, sometimes only the reader is aware of the disparity between what is intended and what happens. At other times, however, the characters themselves also recognize this difference, invariably, of course, when it is too late to change anything. They, therefore, are made to suffer doubly.

CHAPTERS 6-7

Summary

The following Sunday Jude goes to Marygreen to visit his aunt, who is ill. When he reveals he has been seeing Sue the old woman warns him off, and both she and her companion, who looks after her, recall incidents revealing the fact that people in the town thought of Sue as a unique, sometimes unconventional, child. The fact that some of the villagers he meets remind him by their questions of his as yet unaccomplished purpose in going to Christminster causes Jude to take stock of himself.

Practically, he has gotten nowhere; he decides to write to several masters in the colleges for advice. While waiting for replies, he learns that Phillotson is moving to a new school and wonders what this means. Realizing that he will be able to get into the university neither by qualifying for a scholarship nor by buying his way in, Jude considers how he has been seduced by the glamor of Christminster. From a high building he surveys the ancient university which it is not his destiny to be a part of, and he thinks how easily he could have given up his ambitions with Sue as a companion. After drinking at an inn, he goes home, to discover a letter of rejection from one of the masters he has written to. Again, he goes to a bar, later thinking as he walks alone that the real history of the city is in the streets among the common folk, not in the ancient buildings of the colleges. On a wall of the college whose master replied to his letter he scornfully scrawls a verse from Job.

The next day, despairing of both his ambitions and his relationship with Sue, Jude spends the day drinking in a tavern, meeting some of the habitués and loudly leading the criticism of all aspects of university life. Challenged to repeat the Creed in Latin, Jude does so, with the help of drinks the others buy. Disgusted with himself and longing for Sue, he makes his way to Lumsdon and raps on her window. She takes him in and listens to him berate himself as wicked; she insists he get some sleep and promises him breakfast in the morning.

Once awake in the morning, however, Jude is ashamed to face Sue and sneaks away, deciding he will leave Christminster. Discovering he has been dismissed by his employer, he packs his belongings and walks to Marygreen. Once there, he realizes that the ignominy into which he fell with Arabella is not nearly so deep as the abyss in which he now finds himself. Talking of this to the new clergyman who has called on his aunt, he says he is less sad over his inability to get into the university than he is over his losing the chance to get into the church.

Commentary

Hardy represents Jude's sense of failure at Christminster in two ways: from the heights and from the depths, as it were. Jude goes to a place from which he can view the whole city and contemplates the buildings of the colleges from which he is to be excluded. This is the real Christminster he is looking at, but it is the ideal one which has brought him here and from which he feels shut out.

He then descends to the streets and the taverns. Here he drinks, and here it is that he has an opportunity to display his learning, reciting the Creed in Latin for his drinking companions. This recitation is echoed in the last part of the novel when he addresses a street crowd in Christminster, some of whom are now in this scene at the tavern.

As a kind of anticlimax, Jude rushes to Sue in despair, though she can do nothing for him and he leaves again, ashamed. He has been undone again, even as he was by his marriage to Arabella. Later, Jude is to think that women have time and again frustrated his hopes. Hardy suggests throughout that this is but the outward appearance of a cause that is more universal and deeply disturbing.

26

PART THIRD
CHAPTERS 1-2
Summary

Jude believes that his original plan may have come more from ambition than a desire to serve and that his entering the church as a licentiate will enable him both to do good and to purge himself of sin. He does nothing about his new idea until he hears from Sue that she is going to Melchester to a training college, and he decides to go there, work and study, and eventually enter the theological college. He will be near Sue, whom he will learn to love as a friend and will be realizing his new plan. Upon an urgent letter from Sue now at Melchester and lonely and sorry that she let Phillotson persuade her to come, Jude leaves Marygreen for Melchester.

When Jude calls on Sue at the college, he finds her changed in appearance and manner but not in any other way. Determined finally to tell her of his marriage to Arabella, Jude is equally determined to discover the nature of her relationship to Phillotson. After talking about everything else, Sue finally tells Jude she has promised to marry Phillotson at the end of her two years of training. Jude is upset but resolute in his desire to keep seeing her no matter what, certain that his late night visit to her at Lumsdon precipitated her engagement. Jude finds work and lodgings and sets out on his theological study.

During an afternoon together, Jude and Sue visit an old castle, an example of Corinthian rather than Gothic architecture, at Sue's insistence. And they look at the paintings there, Jude preferring religious pictures, Sue secular. At Jude's suggestion they go for a long walk, planning to take a different train back to Melchester but they discover too late they will not be able to make it. Forced to stay overnight with a shepherd, they disagree over Sue's remark that she likes such a rustic life, Jude insisting she is really a city person. They return the next day, and of course Sue has overstayed her leave. Before she leaves him at the college she gives him a new photograph of herself.

Commentary

It is both thematically and dramatically appropriate that after Jude's failure at Christminster he should discover upon meeting Sue again that she is engaged to Phillotson. Failure follows hard upon failure, and Jude's realization that his running to Sue in despair over his having to give up his Christminster dream hastened the engagement makes it no less easy to take. When by chance he is put in the position of staying out overnight with her, he is further reminded that he cannot have what he wants. In short, Hardy is using the scenes here to trace the early stages of Jude's defeat, the frustration of whatever hopes he has.

CHAPTERS 3-5

Summary

At the training college the previous evening there is a good deal of talk about Sue and her young man. The year before a student was seduced by a young man who claimed to be the girl's cousin, so there is some doubt about the fact that Jude is supposed to be Sue's cousin. After Sue does come in the next morning, the girls learn she has been severely punished, and they make a protest, only to learn that inquiries made have revealed Sue has no cousin. That evening they learn that Sue has gone, presumably climbing out of a back window and crossing a river. Sue turns up at Jude's lodgings wet and asking for help. He gives her a suit of his clothes until hers can dry, and after taking some brandy she falls asleep.

When Sue awakens, she and Jude talk through much of the night, the conversation beginning with what Sue has read and why. She says her unusual taste in books came from a Christminster undergraduate with whom she had a "friendly intimacy." She looked upon the two of them as intellectual companions and after she had agreed to live with him in London was surprised that he meant as a mistress. They did live together, and the young man accused her of cruelty in not yielding to him. When Jude says he believes her as innocent as she is unconventional, she replies she has never had a lover and is proud of it, though he says that not all women are like her.

Sue refuses to pray with Jude, his usual evening custom, and goes on to criticize both the religious and intellectual life of Christminster, pointing out that Jude is the very kind of person for whom the colleges were founded. Jude says he can do without Christminster and prefers something "higher"; Sue retorts that she wants something "broader, truer." After Jude says his prayers Sue speaks of the new New Testament she made for herself by rearranging the books into chronological order and decries the attempt to falsify or misrepresent the contents of the Bible. She promises not to disturb his convictions but says she hoped when she met him that he might be the man whom she had always wanted to "ennoble" to "high aims" but he is too traditional. Jude wishes he could see her as other than a woman because she would make a fascinating companion.

In the morning Sue, uncertain as to what she will do and what Phillotson will think, decides to visit a friend near Shaston until her disgrace has been forgotten. Before she leaves, Jude wants to tell her that he has been married and that he loves her, but she guesses the latter and says he mustn't love her. But as soon as she reaches Shaston she writes him, telling him that she has been cruel and that he may love her if he wishes. Not hearing from her for several days Jude goes to Shaston, to discover she has not written him because of the reason for her not being readmitted to the training college it is said she has been intimate with Jude. Sue accuses him of mistreating her by not revealing that he loves her, and though he realizes he is even more to blame because he is married he still doesn't tell her about Arabella. He is puzzled by her annoyance at his saying that of course she can't care about him because of Phillotson. And he is both puzzled and pleased the next day when she writes to ask forgiveness for the way she treated him when he called on her as well as to tell him she would like to see him when she comes to Melchester.

Commentary

Though Hardy's handling of point of view is conventional for his time, it is noteworthy that the first part of Chapter 3 is not told from the point of view of any of the main characters, a practice which he follows in most of the novel. Much of the time, of course, the point of view is appropriately centered in Jude.

Bringing Jude and Sue together, after she flees the training college, enables Hardy further to develop the difference in their views of the world, a difference established earlier in the novel. It is true that Jude and Sue are, in a sense, counterparts, as Jude remarks; they are both sensitive and thoughtful. But Jude is still the conventional Christian in belief, though these beliefs have been little consolation to him in his times of crisis, and Sue is an agnostic, complaining of the way the Bible is falsified. Sue will not join Jude in his prayers, refusing to be a hypocrite, as she puts it. And she explains the way in which she has rearranged her New Testament in chronological order.

She is also critical of the Christminster Jude so much admires. She says that "intellect at Christminster is new wine in old bottles" and that Jude, unable to enter academic life, is the very kind of man for whom the colleges were founded. She professes a freedom of thought which cannot be confined by a university and which she implies she engaged in with her undergraduate friend.

These are the views which will undergo a reversal during the course of the novel, a reversal which is part of the structure of the novel. In this reversal Jude will learn from Sue, who will in turn seem to repudiate what she has taught him. Especially will Jude come to scorn the religious beliefs he once held. Both will increasingly feel their lives manipulated by some force which they cannot explain.

The changes in Jude especially will demonstrate the theme of the novel. Both he and Sue are, of course, caught in the changes which bring into being the modern spirit, one of questioning and doubt.

CHAPTERS 6-7

Summary

In his new position at Shaston Phillotson, though pursuing his work at the school as well as his interest in antiquities, thinks mostly of Sue: saving money to support his future marriage, rereading her letters, looking at photographs of her. Though for a while he has honored Sue's desire that he not visit her frequently at the training college in Melchester, he grows impatient and pays her a visit only to discover she has been expelled. Entering the nearby cathedral, he encounters Jude and from him discovers the truth about the alleged scandal as well as something of Jude's feelings for Sue.

When Jude meets Sue, finding her evasive about whether she has seen Phillotson, he tells her of his marriage to Arabella. Sue is angry because he has thought of himself first in concealing his marriage and has caused her to allow him to love her, and she asks him how he can reconcile this with his religious beliefs. To Jude's insistence that his marriage is the only obstacle between them, she names several, among which is that she would have to love him. As a reason for not telling her of Arabella, Jude mentions the family's lucklessness in marriage, which momentarily frightens them both. They part, pretending they can still be friends.

When Sue writes to Jude that she is going to marry Phillotson soon, Jude wonders if his revealing his marriage to Arabella has hastened her decision, as he feels his visiting her drunk hurried her engagement. Even more upsetting is a second letter asking Jude to give her away at the ceremony, with its mention of him as her nearest "married relation." At Jude's suggestion Sue comes to stay with him so as to marry from his house, and their behavior toward each other is strained. Certain that she is making a mistake in marrying Phillotson, Jude allows Sue to go into the church a few hours before the wedding to see the place where she is to be married, an odd request that she herself acknowledges is characteristic of her. This and, later, the wedding are painful to Jude, and he wonders if she has willfully wanted him to be present. After the wedding and a meal at Jude's lodgings, when the newly married couple are ready to leave Sue hurries back into the house for her handkerchief. She looks at Jude as if to speak but says nothing and hurries out.

Commentary

Jude is here shown to believe that his telling Sue about his marriage to Arabella has helped to hasten Sue's decision to marry Phillotson, just as earlier he believed that his going to her in despair precipitated her engagement. Even if Jude is wrong in both cases, he believes that he is the unwitting cause. Or, perhaps, it strengthens his growing conviction that some inimical power rules his life and makes his best intentions produce results that undermine him.

In his handling of narrative, Hardy uses two devices here. He has Sue and Jude walk arm in arm down the aisle of the church in which she is to marry Phillotson as a kind of ironical comment on the fact that he is not the one who is really marrying her and as a foreshadowing of the fact that though they try many times to marry they never actually will. Hardy also uses here, and elsewhere, letters between Sue and Jude especially to show the difference between Sue in person and Sue as she writes. Even Jude comments on this difference, remarking that she is nicer in her letters than she is in person.

The treatment of Phillotson in the first part of Chapter 6 is an instance of static analysis of a character, which is used only infrequently in the novel. He is shown in his new situation at Shaston, his interests and habits are catalogued, and his personal appearance at this point is described. Part of the reason for the inclusion of this section is, of course, to show what sort of man Sue is shortly to marry. More often than not, however, Hardy uses scenes and contacts between characters to develop his characterizations.

CHAPTERS 8-9

Summary

With Sue gone, Jude finds Melchester oppressive. News that his aunt is ill and an offer from his former employer at Christminster give him excuse to leave. Finding his aunt very ill indeed, he writes to Sue, suggesting she come and offering to meet her on his way back from Christminster. He finds it a city of ghosts and decides not to return there, but before leaving to meet Sue he goes into a tavern, the one where he recited the Creed, for a drink to relieve his depressed feelings. There he encounters Arabella, back from Australia, working as a barmaid. He agrees to meet her later, though it means missing the train and his meeting with Sue. When Jude has no ideas as to arrangements for their separation, at Arabella's suggestion they go to Aldbrickham and spend the night, giving themselves time, according to her, to decide what to do.

Back in Christminster the next day, Arabella tells Jude she married again in Australia and when he is angry about this says she will go back to the other man if Jude won't have her. No sooner has he left Arabella than he encounters Sue, who has come to look for him, thinking he may have started drinking as the result of being in the city where so many of his hopes have been disappointed. They return to Marygreen together, and Jude tries unsuccessfully to find out about her marriage, convinced she is unhappy. But she will say nothing but good of Phillotson, and she is offended, later, when Aunt Drusilla makes derogatory remarks about marriage and about Phillotson as a husband. Out of her hearing, Sue admits to Jude she may have made a mistake but will not discuss the subject further. In the days after her departure Jude tries to discipline himself not to think of his love for her. While still at Marygreen, Jude gets a letter from Arabella announcing that she is joining her second husband in London and will help him run a tavern.

Commentary

In his return to Christminster and in going back to Marygreen with Sue, Jude encounters the past wherever he walks. In Christminster he comes upon the place where Sue once worked, his old lodgings, the stone yard, and finally the tavern where he recited the Creed in Latin. He and Sue pass the Brown House, the house where he and Arabella lived, and the field where he worked as a boy. Each is a reminder to him of some part of his life, and most have more than a single association attached to them.

It is in the tavern in Christminster that Jude encounters Arabella unexpectedly. Hardy has often been criticized for excessive use of coincidence in his handling of plot, and not one but two instances occur here. He meets Arabella, back from Australia, and soon after leaving her the next day comes upon Sue, whom he expects to be in Marygreen. It is true that both encounters occur at dramatically right times: Arabella after Sue's wedding; Sue after he has spent the night with Arabella. However, the appearances in both cases come about as the result of Hardy's desire to demonstrate something in the relationships among the characters rather than the necessities of the plot.

CHAPTER 10

Summary

Back at Melchester, Jude tries to fight against the temptation to visit Sue at Shaston and tries desperately to pursue his study for the ministry. Enlarging his interest in sacred music and eventually joining a choir in a village church nearby, he is greatly moved by a new hymn and thinks that the composer of it must be the kind of man who would understand his own perplexing state of mind. Jude seeks out the composer but discovers he is interested only in money. Coming home from this trip, he discovers Sue has relented and asked him to visit on that very day. Abandoning his attempt to discipline his feelings for her, he writes to arrange to visit as soon as possible.

Commentary

Jude's impulsive visit to the composer turns into another irony. The man who Jude thinks would be best equipped to understand and sympathize with him turns out to be a kind of businessman. He is interested only in money, not the beauty of his music. Jude is an increasingly lonely man, and this attempt to break out of his loneliness comes to nothing, as all such attempts will. It is a part of what is happening to him. Slowly straying away from his old beliefs, he finds himself without any context for his actions and thoughts. Sue is no help here: she is too self-centered, and all she can offer is questions, not answers. All men are like Jude, so Hardy seems to suggest—modern men, at least.

PART FOURTH

CHAPTERS 1-2

Summary

When Jude visits Sue at Shaston, he sits playing his favorite hymn while waiting for her to come in. Her being moved by it causes him to say that at heart they are alike, but Sue counters by saying they are, however, not alike "at head." When they argue over whether they can still be friends, Jude calls her a flirt; she replies by saying that some women can't be satisfied with loving and being loved by only one man. She calls him a Joseph, a Don Quixote, a St. Stephen, and speaks of herself as a woman full of conflicting feelings. Leaving her and wandering about the town while waiting for his train, Jude finally finds his way back to Sue's house, and from the dark sees her inside take out a photograph and clasp it to her bosom but can't be sure if it's his. He knows that he will go see her again, no matter what resolves he makes.

Though Sue writes to say he mustn't come to see her and Jude replies to agree, he does notify her when his aunt dies, expecting Sue to come to Marygreen for the funeral. She does come, and after the funeral she brings up the subject of unhappy marriages and the reasons for them, particularly mentioning a woman's "fastidiousness." When Jude tries to apply her remarks personally she insists she is not unhappy. Purposely, Jude tells her that he has seen Arabella and he may go back to her because of the way Sue has acted toward him. Sue finally does admit she is unhappy but blames it on her own wickedness, though she says that "what tortures [her] so much is the necessity of being responsive to this man whenever he wishes, good as he is morally." Later, when Jude goes outside to put out of its suffering a rabbit caught in a trap, he finds that Sue has been unable to sleep. She says that with his religious beliefs he must think it a sin for her to tell him her troubles, but Jude replies that he will forego all his beliefs if she will let him help her.

Commentary

Jude and Sue are brought together, first at Shaston and then by the aunt's death at Marygreen, in order to make possible a criticism of the institution of marriage. The essential point is that marriage as a social institution is unresponsive to the needs of the individual, and Sue is the spokesman for this view, not only on the basis of her fairly brief experience with Phillotson, but also on the basis of her ideas. She speaks here for the new woman whose "love of being loved is insatiable," as is her "love of loving." She assumes more freedom than, perhaps, she knows what to do with, and her sense of being free is in conflict with what society demands. What

t demands is, of course, commitment or contract until death. As a
character Sue, naturally, is trying to justify her attitude toward
Phillotson as well as Jude, neither of whom is able to make her out.
Jude's response, finally, is his willingness to give up his old notions
of marriage, not because they are wrong, but because he will do
anything for Sue.

This consideration of marriage is continued in the next two
chapters in Sue's comments to Phillotson and Phillotson's to Gillingham. Of the four characters, only Gillingham maintains the
conventional view steadfastly. Even Phillotson changes sufficiently
to allow Sue to leave him, although he says it is against his principles. In short, the old is giving way to the new, though even Sue,
the most outspoken, keeps referring perfunctorily to the fact that
she must be wicked to act toward her husband as she does. She
prefers the idea of freedom to the idea of sin, but the old habits
of thought and the old terminology still persist.

CHAPTERS 3-4

Summary

When Sue leaves, she and Jude kiss passionately; reflecting
on it, Jude sees it as a sign of his alienation from the ministry, an
indication of his being unfit to profess the conventional beliefs. He
thinks of the fact that Arabella hindered his aspirations to knowledge and now Sue has interfered with his desire to enter the
church. He therefore burns all his theological works, so as not to
leave himself in a hypocritical position. Sue berates herself for
being weak but when she sees Phillotson again tells him of Jude's
holding her hand, not his kissing her. That night she sleeps apart
from her husband and the next day asks if she can live away from
him. She tells him that she married him because she could not think
of anything else to do and was frightened by the scandal at the
training college. She argues that "domestic laws should be made
according to temperaments," when Phillotson says her request is
irregular. When he asks what she means by living away from him,
she says she meant living with Jude, not necessarily as his wife,
but in any way she chooses. In a series of notes exchanged be-

tween their classrooms as they teach, Phillotson agrees only to letting her live apart from him in the house.

When one night Phillotson mistakenly enters Sue's room, she leaps out of the window and slightly injures herself, later explaining to her husband that her action was caused by a dream, an explanation he doesn't believe. Phillotson goes to see his teacher friend Gillingham, in a nearby town, to have someone to talk to. Admitting that Jude and Sue "seem to be one person split in two," he tells his friend that he has decided to let Sue go, her jumping out the window being the final sign of her unwillingness to stay with him. Against Gillingham's arguments, Phillotson can only say that his instinct tells him to set Sue free, though it is opposed to all he believes in. He tells Sue of his decision, and on the day she is to leave they discuss only practical matters. After Sue leaves, Gillingham comes to call.

Commentary

Hardy is quite right: the kiss Jude and Sue exchange before she leaves Marygreen is a turning point for him. Very quickly, Jude is shown deciding he must give up a career in the church, and he burns his theological works in the garden of his aunt's house. Returning to Phillotson, Sue sleeps apart from him, asks to live away from him, and very soon is allowed to leave him to go to Jude.

It is a turning point in those relationships which embody the structure of the novel. Jude is giving up any hope for a career: "he was as unfit, obviously, by nature, as he had been by social position to fill the part of a propounder of accredited dogma." And even if he says that he will no longer profess anything although he may believe as before, it is obvious he is reaching the point where he doubts too much to believe as he did. Sue's instruction plus what she means to him has reached a ready pupil. Since he is willing to give up so much for her, to let his emotional life take precedence over his dream of a career, he is ready for her to come to him.

Though Sue believes as she has from the start, perhaps because she does, she is ready to give up a marriage that she has never believed in. That she is ready for a different relationship than that she has had with Jude before is another matter, but giving up on Phillotson, in a sense she has no one but Jude. The radical change in her beliefs comes later.

An interesting aspect of Hardy's narrative method here is the way he shows the deteriorating relationship between Sue and Phillotson. Sue debates with her husband, almost formally, with references to authorities. Their discussion finally collapses into a series of notes exchanged between their classrooms. Their communication is really no communication at all, and it becomes ludicrous.

CHAPTER 5

Summary

Jude meets Sue at Melchester and they go on to Aldbrickham. He tells her Arabella has written to ask him to divorce her so she can remarry her Australian husband; Jude is therefore free. When he tells Sue he has reserved a room for them at a hotel, she protests she can't be intimate with him yet and tries to defend herself by saying she hasn't the courage of her convictions. Angry, Jude says she is incapable of "real love," but she replies that she has trusted Jude "to set [her] wishes above [his] gratification." When Jude says that in spite of her views she is as conventional as anyone, she mentions again a woman's love of being loved and the way this can lead her into unfortunate situations. Needing to find a different hotel, Jude unwittingly takes her to the inn where he spent the night with Arabella, and Sue finds this out from a maid. Though Sue was then supposedly happy with Phillotson and Jude legally married to Arabella, Sue is angry, and Jude complains that she expects too much of him. She is pacified only when she learns that at the time he didn't know Arabella was married to another man. She asks him to repeat some lines from Shelley to flatter her, but when he can't recall them she does so herself.

Commentary

When Sue meets Jude and they go off to Aldbrickham, coincidence puts them in the same inn as the one in which he and Arabella spent a night after Sue's marriage. Even the room Sue has is the same one Jude and Arabella used. Again, it suits Hardy's purposes to have the relationship between Jude and Arabella in the background of this first night after Sue has left Phillotson to come to Jude. But the manipulation of the plot to put the two in this particular place is a little too obvious.

Jude and Sue take separate rooms at the inn, and there is a symbolism of separate rooms running throughout the novel. Sue and her undergraduate live together in London but in separate rooms. When Jude and Sue are on an outing during the time she is in the training college in Melchester, they sleep separately at the shepherd's cottage when they must stay away overnight, though the shepherd first takes them for a married couple. Before Sue comes to Jude, she manifests her repugnance toward Phillotson by insisting they sleep in separate rooms. It is significant, indeed, that now that Sue has fled from her husband she requires of Jude that he sleep apart from her. She tries to justify this demand by arguments that she has used before, and Jude complains as before that she is incapable of "real love." After a year of living together, they will still be found in separate rooms.

In the present scene this symbolic separation is set against the memory of Jude's having shared the room with Arabella. Sue shows that this memory strikes her forcefully and, in a way, is a kind of pressure on her to allow the intimacy Jude wants. Arabella's actual presence later in the novel does, of course, force her to yield to him.

CHAPTER 6

Summary

When Sue does not return to Phillotson and he does not hesitate to tell the school authorities why, he is asked to resign, refuses to do so, and is dismissed. In the public meeting he calls to defend himself, most townspeople are against him, but some few are for him. The scuffle that results turns the meeting into a bad farce. Owing to Gillingham's telling her that he is ill, Sue comes to see Phillotson; he asks her to come back but she will not. He learns for the first time that Jude has been married. Later, he tells Gillingham that for Sue's sake he is going to divorce her, as Jude is divorcing Arabella.

Commentary

The "farcical yet melancholy" scene of the public meeting that Phillotson insists on calling is the only one of its kind in the novel. It occupies only one paragraph, and it is described rather than presented dramatically. But it does have a kind of appropriateness in showing to what a decent man like Phillotson has been reduced.

What the slapstick quality of the scene helps to show is the irony in the fact that with the best of intentions Phillotson has brought about all the difficulties he now finds himself in. He decided to let Sue go though it was against his beliefs; he insists on being honest about why she never returns; he goes out of his way to call a meeting in which to try to defend what he has done. What he now suffers is what Gillingham predicted that he would: public ignominy and scorn. Even worse, the whole thing has collapsed into low comedy. Like Jude, Phillotson is unable to hurt anyone, and again like Jude, with the best will in the world he usually succeeds in hurting himself. In spite of what has happened, he predictably decides he will divorce Sue and give her complete freedom.

PART FIFTH

CHAPTER 1

Summary

A year later at Aldbrickham, Jude and Sue are still living as they were. With Phillotson's divorce from Sue now final, they both are free, Jude's divorce from Arabella having become final some time before. When Jude brings up the subject of their marrying, Sue says she would rather they go on as lovers and avoid the oppressive effects of marriage, though Jude objects that most people marry as a matter of course. Again, he complains of her lack of "animal passion" and her seeming inability to love him, but she

40

still wants to dictate the terms of their relationship and Jude acquiesces. With some assistance from Sue, Jude is doing work on headstones, "a lower class of handicraft" than his cathedral work previously.

Commentary

In addition to using frequently a series of short scenes to develop his narrative, Hardy sometimes falls into awkwardness when it is necessary to indicate a passage of time. This chapter begins: "How Gillingham's doubts were disposed of will most quickly appear by passing over the series of dreary months and incidents that followed the events of the last chapter, and coming on to a Sunday in the February of the year following." It is hardly a felicitous transition. In fact, this sentence might well be omitted, and the chapter open with the paragraph that follows.

In the conversation which occurs in this chapter, which presents briefly the state of the relationship established between Jude and Sue since they have been living together, Sue complains that Jude is "too sermony" in the way he speaks. The same might be said about other conversation in the novel. At times Jude and Sue especially seem to make speeches to each other rather than converse.

CHAPTERS 2-3

Summary

When Arabella calls on Jude and Sue, he discovers she is not married; she tells him that she has something important to discuss with him. When Sue urges him not to go out with Arabella because she isn't his wife, Jude replies that neither is Sue. When he returns soon, not having found Arabella in the street, Sue again implores him not to go to her. Though Jude admits his weaknesses, he is bitter about denying himself for nothing. Faced with a choice, Sue gives in to Jude, saying she will marry him, will allow the intimacy he has so strongly desired; and Jude does not go out looking for Arabella.

The next morning Jude talks of starting arrangements for their marriage, and Sue goes to see Arabella. She quickly sees that Sue possesses Jude in a way she didn't yesterday and says her visit probably helped it along. She receives a telegram from her Australian husband in which he agrees to marry her, a circumstance she has brought about by telling him Jude might take her back. Arabella tells Sue that she will write to Jude about the important matter she came to discuss.

Though Jude and Sue start out to the parish clerk's, they decide to delay putting up the banns for their marriage, Sue saying Arabella's remarks about matrimony have reminded her of the oppressiveness of such an obligation. Arabella's letter arrives, announcing that she is married to Cartlett and that she wants Jude to look after their son, born soon after her arrival in Australia. Jude is willing to look after the child, whether or not it actually is his, and Sue agrees, suggesting maybe they should now marry. The boy arrives by himself from London, sent on by Arabella after he leaves the ship from Australia, and comes to Jude and Sue. Sue says she sees Jude in the boy and allows him to call her mother.

Commentary

With Sue's giving herself to Jude, they are now "married," though they will never be joined in any ceremony recognized by society. This "marriage" is significant in several ways for the structure of the novel. Jude has strayed far from the conventional beliefs he held at the beginning of the novel, largely through the influence of Sue. And though each has been married to another, they are legally free and are living together as husband and wife. The relationship is not exactly what either one has wanted, but they are together.

That Sue's giving herself to Jude is brought about by Arabella's presence is an irony even Arabella is conscious of. In a sense, Sue is made to compete with Arabella at her own level or, to put it fairly, at the level at which any woman must compete for a man. Though she does so unwillingly, Sue wants to keep Jude from Arabella. The further irony is, of course, that even with this concession on Sue's part Arabella will eventually win, in a sense.

42

That this and other events in the novel may be brought about by some threatening power that controls man's destiny is symbolized in the appearance of Jude's child, Little Father Time. He makes his appearance as "Age masquerading as Juvenility," and everything about him suggests that he is meant to be more than a child. In fact, there is never much about him that suggests he is a child. That he should appear soon after Sue gives herself to Jude, an important event in the novel, is certainly no coincidence.

Jude's allusion to Job, "Let the day perish wherein I was born," is one of several throughout the novel. Jude remarks here that some day his son may find himself saying this; but, of course, it is Jude himself who repeats this very passage from Job before he dies. The symbol of Job is an appropriate one for Jude: he suffers much, and it is never given to him to know why.

CHAPTER 4

Summary

The morning after the boy arrives, Jude and Sue discover he is called Little Father Time because, as he says, he looks so old. Jude and Sue give notice of their wedding and invite Mrs. Edlin, the widow who took care of his aunt, to come. The night before they are to marry, Mrs. Edlin tells a tale about a man hanged near the Brown House, a man who may have been an ancestor of Sue and Jude. The next day they go to marry at the registry office, but after watching other couples, first Sue and then Jude decide the setting is too sordid. They go to a parish church to watch a wedding, but they agree they can't go through with a ceremony like that they both experienced before. They decide that the compulsion of marriage is not for such as they, and Sue says, "If we are happy as we are, what does it matter to anybody?"

Commentary

These scenes make clear that Jude and Sue will never submit their relationship to the forms of society. In the registry office and in a church they watch others marry, just as before Sue's marriage to Phillotson they walk down the aisle of the church in a pretense of marriage. More important is the reason for their not going through with marriage. Sue says it is as if "a tragic doom" guided the destiny of their family in this respect. The idea that something outside their lives frustrates everything they do will come into their thoughts more and more, and of course is symbolized in the figure of Little Father Time. It has been in the background from the beginning of the novel but comes to the fore in this living symbol.

This idea is echoed in the tale Mrs. Edlin tells of the man hanged near the Brown House. Mrs. Edlin, who in her person and in her sense of family history is very much a part of the Wessex landscape, is used here to illustrate the idea of the doomed family.

CHAPTER 5

Summary

At the agricultural show at Stoke-Barehills Arabella, arriving with her husband, sees Jude, Sue, and the boy and follows after them, commenting on them to Cartlett. Leaving him to go his own way, Arabella encounters a girl friend and then Physician Vilbert. They follow Jude and Sue to the art department, where the couple view a model of one of the Christminster colleges they have made. Arabella jokingly buys a "love-philtre" from Vilbert and then goes off to join her husband. Meanwhile at the pavilion of flowers Sue ecstatically admires the roses, and she and Jude agree they are happy, though conscious of the gloomy face of Little Father Time beside them.

Commentary

The scenes at the agricultural show are used primarily to show Jude and Sue as seen through Arabella's eyes. Arabella is never far away from them and never gives up her desire to get Jude back; though she married Cartlett, it was only a way of providing for herself at the time. She is shrewd enough to see what others do not, and Jude and Sue themselves are unable to: "I am inclined to think that she don't care for him quite so much as he does for her." Of course, this observation is colored by the fact that she wants to believe that she can get Jude back; nevertheless, what she sees is true.

The way in which Little Father Time is used as a symbol is shown at the end of this chapter. Sue has been admiring some roses, and she and Jude have agreed that they are happy. They are, however, concerned about the fact that the child is not enjoying himself. The boy understands this and says, "I should like the flowers very much, if I didn't keep on thinking they'd be all withered in a few days." It is impossible to believe that a child his age would say this. And it demonstrates why this particular symbol fails. It is too obvious, and the child is made to represent more significance than he is naturally capable of doing. A symbol like that of Christminster, on the other hand, does not suffer from these shortcomings.

CHAPTER 6

Summary

To stop the talk about them, Jude and Sue go off to London for a few days as if to marry, but the talk continues and Jude thinks they should move to where they are unknown. Several incidents confirm this idea: Jude loses a job at a church when, because of Sue's presence there, he is recognized and the rumors about them are repeated; Little Father Time is taunted at school by other boys; Jude feels pressured to resign from the committee governing an artisans' improvement society he belongs to. Since they plan to live in lodgings instead of a house and also since they need money, Jude auctions off most of their household effects. They aren't sure where they'll go, but not to London, and since Jude is dissatisfied with church work he isn't sure what he'll do. Sue is upset by the sale of her pet pigeons, turns them loose later at the shop of the poulterer who bought them, and remarks bitterly, "O why should Nature's law be mutual butchery!"

Commentary

Jude and Sue are shown to suffer one setback after another: people are uncivil to them; Little Father Time is harassed at school; Jude's work diminishes; he loses a job at a church when Sue is recognized; he resigns from the committee of a workmen's educational society he belongs to under unspoken pressure from other members. They decide to move to where they are not known, and since they must take lodgings instead of a house they auction their household goods. The implication is that all this is happening to them because of that malign power that operates to frustrate man's hopes. Or it may be that society retaliates against those who violate the rules it sets down. But the former is more strongly suggested.

As Sue says, it is "droll" and ironical that she and Jude should be working to restore the Ten Commandments in the church. Neither in belief nor in action do they subscribe to the meaning of these rules.

CHAPTERS 7-8

Summary

Two and a half years pass, and Jude and Sue are living at Kennetbridge, not far from Marygreen, Jude having worked in many places over the years and still unchanged in his refusal to work on churches. During the time of the spring fair, Arabella comes with her friend Anny for the dedication of a new chapel and encounters Sue, who is selling cakes and gingerbreads at a stall. Arabella tells Sue her husband is dead and questions her about her life. She says that she is married, that she has two children (she is pregnant with a third), that Jude has lost his pride, is ill, and bakes cakes because he can do the work indoors. The fact that the cakes are in shapes reminiscent of buildings at Christminster causes both women to agree that Jude still thinks of the city as his ideal. Arabella tells Sue that since her husband's death she has found religion, and she has come from Alfredston, where she lives with her friend, for the dedication.

On her way home from Kennetbridge Arabella tells her friend Anny that she wishes she had Jude back, that he is more hers than Sue's, and that she won't be a hypocrite any longer about religion. Along the way, they meet Phillotson, now teaching at Marygreen again, and Arabella identifies herself, this being the first time they have met since Arabella was his pupil. Telling him where Sue now is, Arabella criticizes Phillotson for letting her go, pointing out that Sue was never initimate with Jude before the divorce. She lectures him on how he should treat a wife.

46

In Kennetbridge, when Sue returns to their lodgings, she tells Jude she has sold all the cakes and has seen Arabella. Jude takes Arabella's living near as a good enough reason for moving on and to Sue's surprise says he wants to return to Christminster, which he loves even though he knows it despises men like him. Accordingly, in a few weeks they go.

Commentary

Jude and Sue are reduced to living off the sale of the cakes and gingerbreads Jude bakes. The fact that they are made in the shapes of buildings at Christminster not only reveals that it is a "fixed vision" with him, as Sue says, but foreshadows his return there. Having aimlessly gone from one town to another for several years in pursuit of work, Jude will finally return to the place of his youthful dream as if to die there.

Arabella's meeting with Phillotson, coincidental though it may be, makes the final connection among the main characters, since they are the only two who have never met in recent years. Here and later, she reports to Phillotson on the state of the relationship between Sue and Jude; her motives are, of course, selfish.

PART SIXTH

CHAPTERS 1-2

Summary

Jude has planned it so they arrive on Remembrance Day (anniversary of founding of the university), and instead of looking for lodgings he wants to view the festivities. But when he sees young men from the colleges, he feels it will be "Humiliation Day" for him. He passes the building from which he looked out over the colleges and decided he would never achieve his academic ambitions, and he is recognized by several men with whom he drank and who now remind him of his failure. He addresses a speech to them and the crowd, in which he discusses his attempt to succeed and the reasons for failure, ending with the declaration that "there is something wrong somewhere in our social formulas." In their wanderings through the crowds Sue has spotted Phillotson, an indication to her that he must live somewhere near. They have a difficult time finding lodgings for the whole family, finally settling for rooms for Sue and the children only. When the landlady discovers Sue is not married, she tells her husband and informs Sue she must leave the next day. With Little Father Time she looks unsuccessfully for another place but decides not to worry Jude with the problem until the next day.

In the bare rooms from which Sue can see some of the colleges, a proximity Jude has insisted on, Sue talks to Little Father Time before they go to bed. The boy is sure the family's plight is caused by the children and can't understand why children are born at all, though Sue explains to him it is a law of nature. When she tells him she is pregnant with another child, he says she has done it on purpose to bring the family to further ruin. The next morning, without looking in on the children she goes to find Jude and tells him of their problem about lodgings. When they return to Sue's lodgings to prepare breakfast for the children, she goes into their room, to discover all three are dead. Jude and Sue decide, when they think about it later, that Little Father Time awakened to find Sue gone, hanged the two younger children first and then hanged himself. The note he left seems to confirm this.

To comfort Sue, Jude repeats the doctor's observation that Little Father Time is one of a new generation of children with a preternatural wisdom and sense of defeat. Sue, not relieved, speaks of a fate that has ruled their lives inexorably, says that in dealing with the boy she should have been wiser, and remembers with dismay that once she asserted they should enjoy the instincts nature gave them. Jude agrees that a fate rules and that they can do nothing about their destiny. Jude doesn't allow Sue to attend the funeral; however, when he returns from it he discovers she is gone and finds her at the grave, insisting the gravedigger stop filling in the grave so she can look at her dead children. Jude takes her home, puts her to bed, and calls the doctor; her baby is prematurely born dead.

Commentary

The two important scenes here embody the theme of the novel rather directly. Jude's speech to the street crowd is his second public performance, the other being his recitation in a tavern of the Creed in Latin. Here he tries to explain his life. He asserts that his failure is a failure of circumstances (poverty), not will; but later he remarks, "I was, perhaps, after all, a paltry victim to the spirit of mental and social restlessness, that makes so many unhappy in these days!" But Sue will not allow this and says he "struggled nobly to acquire knowledge." After admitting he is in "a chaos of principles" now, he ends by remarking that something is wrong with society. In short, Jude acknowledges that he has been caught in changes he doesn't understand and has ended not knowing what to believe in.

That "something external" to them, as Sue puts it with Jude agreeing by reference to a line from *Agamemnon,* should have shaped their destiny is vividly suggested in the melodramatic scene of the children's death. Suddenly, Little Father Time and the other two are gone, and Sue's child is born dead. Without reason, as far as Jude and Sue can see, this last blow is dealt them.

The scene is one of those sensational, melodramatic incidents for the use of which in his novels critics have often taken Hardy to task. Perhaps such scenes can be justified on the basis of the fact that most of his novels were first serialized in magazines and he needed to maintain reader interest from month to month. Whatever the reason for their inclusion, here the scene is impossible to believe, not the least of the reasons for which is the note Little Father Time leaves, "Done because we are too menny." Further, the scene is inconsistent with the kind of reality Hardy depicts everywhere else in the novel.

The unreality of the scene is increased because the chief actor in it is Little Father Time. It is appropriate to his symbolic meaning that he should be the one to hang the two children before, of course, taking his own life. As one critic has pointed out, Little Father Time as a symbol is unnecessary because what he stands for is already illustrated in Jude's own life.

It is of course significant that these scenes occur in Christminster, Jude's symbol of all that is good in life.

CHAPTERS 3-4

Summary

During her convalescence Sue says she is beaten and must conform, and Jude asserts he belongs to "that vast band of men shunned by the virtuous—the men called seducers." She still feels she belongs to Phillotson. Jude is aware of the fact that he and Sue are going in opposite directions: she is returning to the conventional ideas she taught Jude to abandon. She insists that now she must practice "self-renunciation," but Jude argues that she has only acted out of natural instincts. She has been attending church frequently, Jude finds out, and does not want to be criticized for doing so. She doesn't want to go through the marriage ceremony with him because she feels she is still married to Phillotson. When Arabella calls, having come to Christminster to look at her son's grave, Sue insists that she is not Jude's wife. After Sue mysteriously leaves, Arabella says she is living at Alfredson with her father, now back from Australia. Jude looks for Sue, finally discovering her in church. She tells him that Arabella's child killing hers is a judgment on her. They disagree over whether she is his wife, Jude arguing that their marriage was made by nature, Sue that it was not made in heaven as hers to Phillotson was.

Jude cannot understand how Sue can have changed so, but she is convinced she has seen the light at last. She doesn't want him to return to their lodgings, but he does anyway. A conversation ensues in which each tries to take the blame for the relationship between them: Jude says he shouldn't have forced her into intimacy, though he still complains she hasn't felt for him what he feels for her; she admits she tried to attract him and through envy of Arabella gave herself to him in order to hold him. She insists they part, though Jude tries to convince her that he needs her as a defense against his weaknesses. She tells him that they must separate not because she dislikes him but because her conscience says it's right, and she suggests they can still be friends as they used to be.

After seeing Jude and Sue in Christminster on Remembrance Day, Phillotson reads of the death of the children in a newspaper while in Alfredston. Encountering Arabella there, he learns from her that Jude and Sue aren't living together, that they have never married, that Sue considers herself Phillotson's wife, and that Little Father Time was really Arabella's child. He decides to ask Sue to return to him, realizing what positive effects it might have on other aspects of his life, and writes her a letter. In Christminster Sue calls on Jude to tell him she has decided to return to Phillotson, to remarry him, and she suggests Jude go back to Arabella. Jude cannot understand this extreme penance on Sue's part. She purposely walks with him to the cemetery so they can say goodbye over the graves of the children.

Commentary

Jude and Sue are shown in the scenes here to have reached the point at which their beliefs have reversed. The structure of the novel is such that the next step is for them to dissolve their relationship, with Sue the instigator. Sue now talks about the necessity of "self-renunciation" and the feeling that she still belongs to Phillotson. Jude argues that she was simply following her natural instincts in coming to him and that theirs is "Nature's own marriage." But Sue answers that it was not made in heaven, as was hers with Phillotson. The change in Sue is shown further in her attending church almost daily and in her conviction that Arabella's child killing hers was a judgment on her.

It is not surprising, then, that she accepts Phillotson's offer to return to him and remarry. It will be the right thing to do and will serve as a penance for her sins. She even suggests that Jude make things right by returning to Arabella.

CHAPTER 5

Summary

Sue goes to Marygreen and Phillotson's house, and when Phillotson greets her with a kiss she shrinks from him. The wedding is to be the next day, and she is to stay with Mrs. Edlin. When Sue refuses to wear an attractive nightgown, indeed destroys it, Mrs.

Edlin tells her she still loves Jude and shouldn't marry Phillotson. Phillotson discusses his reasons for wanting to marry Sue with Gillingham and says so much about the way a man should govern a wife that his friend wonders if he will not be too hard on Sue. Mrs. Edlin embarrasses Phillotson by coming to tell him that Sue is forcing herself to marry him and he shouldn't go through with it, but Gillingham assures him he is right to marry her. Phillotson and Sue are married in the church the next morning, and afterward at home he tells her he will respect her "personal privacy" as he did before.

Commentary

Every detail in these scenes shows Sue is forcing herself to remarry Phillotson as a penance: she shrinks from his kiss; she is startled by seeing the marriage license; she destroys a nightgown she bought for Jude's sake and insists on wearing a plain one; she cries; she wants the marriage performed quickly.

Here and in the previous section Phillotson is shown to be acting on the basis of expediency in taking Sue back. He has decided it might improve his standing in the community and in his profession, and to Gillingham he mouths conventional advice about how a husband should govern his wife. In short, his motives for taking her back are less admirable than those for letting her go. Of course, he has suffered a good deal from allowing her to leave him for Jude.

CHAPTERS 6-7

Summary

In Christminster Arabella comes to Jude's lodgings, saying she has nowhere to go and asking him to take her in. Eventually he does give her a place to sleep, and when she asks him if he knows of the wedding, he is irritable about the subject. Another day, she offers to find out if the wedding actually took place when she goes to Alfredston. Upon her return she tells Jude that Sue and Phillotson are married, that Sue burned her good nightgown to forget Jude, that Sue thought Phillotson her only husband, and that she feels that way with respect to Jude. While Jude goes to a tavern to drink, Arabella arranges with her father, now living in the city, to bring Jude there that night. Finding Jude, Arabella encourages him in his

52

drinking and later guides him to her father's house, Jude drunk enough not to be sure where he is.

The next day Arabella arranges with her father to keep Jude in the house until she can get him to marry her, one means of which is a sufficient supply of liquor. She brings his things from his lodgings so he can have no reason to go back there, and has her father give a party to entertain Jude and, supposedly, to advertise his pork shop. After the party, which includes some of Jude's former drinking companions, has been going on a long time, Arabella says it's time for Jude to carry out his promise to marry her; and when Jude says he doesn't remember any promise her father questions his honor. Saying he has never acted dishonorably to anyone, Jude goes off with Arabella and her father to be married. Upon their return Arabella triumphantly describes the wedding, and Jude says he has acted honorably and also done what Sue suggested.

Commentary

Both Jude and Sue have remarried; they have conformed. But the scenes depicting both ceremonies make clear that they are honoring the letter and not the spirit of the institution. As Jude says later, when they remarried he was "gin-drunk" and she was "creed-drunk." Or as he bitterly says here about his remarrying of Arabella, "It is true religion!"

The ceremonies are rather similar. They are held at a time when no one will pay much attention to what is going on. In each case, the officiating clergyman congratulates the couple on having done the right thing and says they ought to be forgiven now.

The marital relationships have come full circle now. Jude and Sue are back with the partners they began with, but for each it is a defeat.

CHAPTERS 8-9
Summary

Jude and Arabella are as incompatible now as they were the first time they were married, she complaining about his always being ill and he wishing he were dead. When Jude asks her to write to Sue

for him, inviting her to visit, Arabella insults Sue, and he is violent
with her but admits he couldn't kill her. Convinced that Arabella
has never mailed the letter she wrote, Jude goes to Marygreen in
spite of his ill health. When Sue congratulates him for marrying
Arabella, he bitterly attacks the way she has changed and tells her
she isn't worth loving. She tells him she has not given herself to
Phillotson and she loves him; they embrace passionately. When he
suggests they run away together, she tells him to leave. He does,
passing for the last time the fields where he chased rooks and the
ridge-track near the Brown House where so much has happened,
even stopping to feel at the back of the milestone the carving he
made there. He is back in Christminster late at night.

Arabella awaits Jude at the station, and he tells her he has accomplished the only two things he now wants: to see Sue and to
die. As she takes him home past the walls of the colleges, he thinks
he sees the eminent men of the past as he did when he first came to
Christminster, but now they seem to laugh at him.

At Marygreen Sue tells Mrs. Edlin that Jude has been there,
that she still loves him, and that she must now perform the most
severe penance, going to Phillotson's bed. Though she asks Mrs.
Edlin to stay overnight in the house because she is afraid, she goes
to Phillotson, wakes him, and asks him to allow her to come in.
She confesses Jude visited and they kissed, but she swears on a New
Testament she will never see him again. Phillotson forgives her,
and though she at first shrinks from his touch she does take his kiss
without reaction.

Commentary

In both Marygreen and Christminster, Jude encounters for the
last time those features of the setting that have been meaningful
to him: the field where he scared rooks, the Brown House, the milestone; the buildings of the colleges, the ghosts of the great men of
the past, who now seem to be laughing at him. He himself seems to
be conscious of a farewell.

Jude's desire to run away with Sue and her decision to go to
Phillotson's bed measure the extremes of the reversals in belief

which have occurred in the two characters. This plus the change in marital relationships shows the structure of the novel moving to its completion. Neither character is as he was in the beginning, and both are seen to go down to defeat.

That they should declare their love for each other after their remarriages makes for a large irony in the novel. Jude's taunt, "Sue, Sue, you are not worth a man's love!" forces Sue momentarily to forget the penance she is determined to make. But it is too late for anything to change. The inexplicable power that has guided their lives so far, hinted at so often in the novel, makes their declarations merely acts of desperation.

CHAPTER 10
Summary

Jude often muses on "the defeat of his early aims" and thinks of the possible changes in the colleges to benefit people like himself. Though he tells Arabella he doesn't want Sue to know about him, when Mrs. Edlin calls he asks about Sue and is startled to discover she is now sharing her husband's bed. He talks about the best days of the relationship between Sue and himself and the ways in which each of them changed. Physician Vilbert, who has been attending Jude at Arabella's request, calls, but Jude's insults cause him to leave. On his way out he meets Arabella, who gives him wine with some of the quack doctor's own "love-philter" in it. From her allowing him to kiss her and from what she says, it is evident that Arabella is keeping an eye out for the time when Jude will be dead.

Commentary

As these brief scenes show, Jude has only the past; to Arabella belong the present and future. Jude is still trying to justify or understand the meaning of his life, this time to Mrs. Edlin: "Our ideas were fifty years too soon to be any good to us. And so the resistance they met with brought reaction in her, and recklessness and ruin on me!" This remark, of course, echoes what he said earlier in his speech to the street crowd.

Meanwhile, Arabella is flirting with Physician Vilbert. When Jude's gone, she'll need someone to take care of her, and she has to take what she can get now.

CHAPTER 11

Summary

On Remembrance Day Arabella, impatient to be off to the festivities, leaves Jude asleep and alone. He awakens, asks for water, recognizes what holiday it is, and repeats some verses from Job. Later, Arabella breaks away long enough to look in on Jude, who she discovers is dead. She rejoins the holiday, eventually meeting Physician Vilbert. She does finally leave him to see about arrangements for Jude's funeral. Two days later, only Arabella and Mrs. Edlin stand by Jude's coffin; the sounds of the holiday come from outside. Mrs. Edlin doesn't know if Sue will come to the funeral but asserts that Sue has said she's found peace. Arabella says that Jude didn't want Sue sent for and did not forgive her and that Sue will never find peace until she is dead like Jude.

Commentary

In the city which is the symbol of his hopes Jude dies, and his death comes on Remembrance Day, which is particularly meaningful to him. His last words are some verses from Job, that symbol that has been used frequently in the novel: "Let the day perish wherein I was born...." Jude has earlier wondered if his own son wouldn't one day repeat these very verses.

There is, of course, irony everywhere in these closing scenes. Certainly there is in the fact that Jude should die in Christminster. Certainly too, there is in the fact that Arabella should have the last word in the novel. About Sue she says, "She's never found peace since she left his arms, and never will again till she's as he is now!" In a way, only Arabella of the four principal characters survives. Jude is dead; Sue is doing penance for what she thinks of as her sins and, according to Mrs. Edlin, has aged greatly; Phillotson, devoid of hope, is back at Marygreen where he began, living with a wife whom he requires to swear loyalty to him on a New Testament.

Ironically too, Arabella has been the least ambitious of all the main characters. The others have been caught up in the spirit of the times and for reasons that seem inexplicable and out of their control have been defeated in their attempts to realize their aspirations.

ANALYSES OF MAIN CHARACTERS

JUDE FAWLEY

Jude is obscure in that he comes from uncertain origins, struggles largely unnoticed to realize his aspirations, and dies without having made any mark on the world. He is also obscure in the sense of being ambiguous: he is divided internally, and the conflicts range all the way from that between sexual desire and knowledge to that between two different views of the world. Jude is, therefore, struggling both with the world and with himself.

He is not well equipped to win. Though he is intelligent enough and determined, he tries to force his way to the knowledge he wants. Though well-intentioned and goodhearted, he often acts impulsively on the basis of too little objective evidence. Though he is unable to hurt an animal or another human being, he shows very little concern for himself and his own survival, often needlessly sacrificing his own good. He never learns, as Phillotson finally does perhaps too late, to calculate how to get what he wants. In short, he is more human than divine, as Hardy points out.

He is obsessed with ideals. Very early he makes Christminster into an ideal of the intellectual life, and his admitted failure there does not dim the luster with which it shines in his imagination to the very end of his life. He searches for the ideal woman who will be both lover and companion, and though he finds passion without intellectual interests in Arabella and wide interests but frigidity in Sue he maintains the latter as his ideal to his deathbed. Recognizing the Christminster holiday just before he dies, Jude says, "And I here. And Sue defiled!"

Jude is reconciled to his fate before he dies only in the sense that he recognizes what it is. In a conversation with Mrs. Edlin he says that perhaps he and Sue were ahead of their time in the way they wanted to live. He does not regret the struggle he has made; at the least, as he lies ill he tries to puzzle out the meaning of his life. At the very end, however, like Job he wonders why he was born. But then so perhaps does every man, Hardy seems to imply.

SUE BRIDEHEAD

It is easy for the modern reader to dislike Sue, even, as D. H. Lawrence did, to make her into the villain of the book. (Lawrence thought Sue represented everything that was wrong with modern women.) Jude, as well as Hardy, obviously sees her as charming, lively, intelligent, interesting, and attractive in the way that an adolescent girl is. But it is impossible not to see other sides to her personality: she is self-centered, wanting more than she is willing to give; she is intelligent but her knowledge is fashionable and her use of it is shallow; she is outspoken but afraid to suit her actions to her words; she wants to love and be loved but is morbidly afraid of her emotions and desires.

In short, she is something less than the ideal Jude sees in her; like him she is human. She is also a nineteenth-century woman who has given herself more freedom than she knows how to handle. She wants to believe that she is free to establish a new sort of relationship to men, even as she demands freedom to examine new ideas. But at the end she finds herself in the role of sinner performing penance for her misconduct. As Jude says, they were perhaps ahead of their time.

If she is not an ideal, she is the means by which Jude encounters a different view of life, one which he comes to adopt even as she flees from it. She is also one of the means by which Jude's hopes are frustrated and he is made to undergo suffering and defeat. But it is a frustration which he invites or which is given him by a power neither he nor Sue understands or seems to control.

ARABELLA DONN

Arabella is the least complex of the main characters; she is also the least ambitious, though what she wants she pursues with determination and enterprise. What she is after is simple enough: a man who will satisfy her and who will provide the comforts and some of the luxuries of life. She is attractive in an overblown way, good-humored, practical, uneducated of course but shrewd, cunning, and tenacious. She is common in her tastes and interests. She is capable of understanding a good deal in the emotional life of other people, especially women, as shown on several occasions with Sue.

Arabella never quite finds what she wants either. Jude's ambitions put her off when they are first married, but after him Cartlett is obviously a poor substitute, though she doesn't complain. She wants Jude again and gets him, but she isn't satisfied, since he is past the point of being much good to her.

That she is enterprising is demonstrated everywhere in the novel; she has a self-interest that amounts to an instinct for survival, rather than the self-interest of a Sue that is the same as pride. And, of course, she does survive intact in a way the others don't. Though at the end of the novel she is standing by Jude's coffin, Vilbert awaits her somewhere in the city. Life goes on, in short.

RICHARD PHILLOTSON

Phillotson is eminently the respectable man. Though he fails to achieve the same goals Jude pursues, his bearing and view of things do not change much. Even when Arabella encounters him on the road to Alfredston, now down on his luck and teaching at Marygreen because it's the only place that will have him, this air of respectability remains. It must be this which Sue can't stand about him, the respectability plus the legal right to make love to her.

Sue's opinion of him does not make him any less decent. He is like Jude in many ways: he is goodhearted and honorable; he allows instinct to overrule reason; he is too accommodating for his own good; he is intelligent. Like Jude he is ill-equipped to get what he wants in life and soon resigns himself to mediocrity. However, unlike Jude he no longer is dazzled by ideals, perhaps because he is older. Maybe too late he learns to act on the basis of calculation, estimating that Sue's return will be worth the benefits it may bring.

Phillotson, in short, is a man whom it is easy neither to like nor to dislike; he goes largely unnoticed.

CRITICAL ANALYSIS

THEME

In no other novel by Hardy is theme so important. And his theme here may be stated briefly as follows: man is becoming aware that his life is governed by old ideas and old institutions and he desires to break out of these obsolete forms. This modern spirit causes him to question old beliefs and institutions and to seek new ones, to give up what is known and tried for the unknown and new, and hence to experience loneliness and frustration as he searches on his own. Specifically in the novel, Hardy depicts characters who raise questions about such things as religious beliefs, social classes, the conventions of marriage, and elite educational institutions and who feel in the absence of the old certainties that the universe may be governed by a mysterious, possibly malign power. Some critics have suggested that Hardy had in mind when he wrote the novel Matthew Arnold's comments on the coming of the modern spirit.

POINT OF VIEW

The most noteworthy thing about Hardy's use of point of view is that it is conventional for his time. He uses a shifting third person point of view which is usually centered in Jude but sometimes is moved to one of the other main characters. Historically, then, Hardy makes no use of the development of point of view as a technique carried out by his contemporary Henry James.

SETTING

Though in this novel Hardy makes less significant use of his Wessex landscape, as well as its customs, superstitions, humor, and human types, than he does in other novels, it is of some importance. Almost all the characters are deeply rooted in and responsive to place, as shown, for example, in Jude's sense of all that has happened on the ridge-track near the Brown House outside Marygreen. Characters like Drusilla Fawley or Mrs. Edlin are very much a product of the area, the aunt with her references to family history, the widow with her comments about marriage. But Hardy's desire to work out his theme seems to override most of this local reference.

PLOT

Hardy's narrative technique has often been criticized. He characteristically uses a succession of short scenes to move the plot forward instead of longer scenes developed in detail. Sometimes his transitions are awkward, especially in the way in which he summarizes the passage of time. He relies frequently on coincidence to bring together characters he wants to have meet. And now and again he indulges in a sensational, melodramatic scene.

Such shortcomings are to be found in this novel, but in Hardy's defense it should be said that he can develop a scene skillfully, he does use contrasting scenes with good effect in forwarding the plot, and he is capable of foreshadowing events in the novel with competence. It may be that his weaknesses in narrative technique come in part from the demands of serial publication; it may also be that he had less interest in this aspect of fiction than he did in others.

STRUCTURE

The structure of the novel might be described as the reversals of belief in Jude and Sue and their changing marital relationships as they both go down to defeat. In the beginning Sue's view of things is secular and rationalist, expressed, for example, in her sympathy with ancient rather than medieval culture, her scorn of conventional religious belief, her buying of pagan statuary, her reading of Gibbon. Jude's beliefs are, at first, conventionally Christian, as his desire to be ordained, his reading of standard authors, and his love of medieval culture and architecture show. By the end of the novel Sue has reverted to conventional beliefs, as evidenced by her concern for the sanctity of marriage and her desire to perform penances for her sins. On the other hand, Jude no longer professes his old beliefs and finds himself, as he says in his speech to the street crowd in Christminster, in "a chaos of principles."

This change in beliefs is closely paralleled by their marital relationships. At first, they are separated by marriage to other people as they are apart in belief. As Jude's ideas change, they are legally freed by divorce, and they come to live together and to be "married," in fact, if not in name. When Sue returns to conventional Christian beliefs, they separate and remarry their first spouses.

Jude's death as a failure in Christminster and Sue's forcing herself to go to Phillotson's bed are striking signs of their defeat in life. This defeat is mirrored as well in Phillotson, who at Mary-green has fallen to the bottom professionally and who stiffly re-quires Sue to swear loyalty to him on a New Testament, and to a lesser extent in Arabella, who though she loses Jude does not lose her vitality.

In these changes and defeat Hardy has embodied the theme of his novel: Jude and Sue have been caught up in the modern spirit, have struggled to break free of the old ways, and have suffered and failed. It is this that justifies Hardy's description of the novel, in his preface to it, as a "tragedy of unfulfilled aims."

SYMBOLISM

The symbolism in the novel helps to work out the theme. Such a minor symbol as the repeated allusion to Samson and Delilah reinforces the way Jude's emotional life undermines the realiza-tion of his ambitions. Two symbols of major importance are Christ-minster and the character of Little Father Time. They are useful to discuss, since the first is an instance of a successful symbol and the second an unsuccessful one.

Jude's idea of Christminster permeates not only his thinking but the whole novel. From his first view of it on the horizon to his hearing the sounds of the holiday there coming in his window as he lies on his deathbed, Christminster represents to him all that is desirable in life. It is by this ideal that he measures everything. He encounters evidence in abundance that it is not in fact what he thinks it is in his imagination, but he will not take heed. It finally represents to him literally all that he has left in life. Of course, other characters as well are affected by Jude's idea of the place. It is a successful symbol because it is capable of representing what it is supposed to and it does not call attention to itself as a literary de-vice.

Little Father Time, however, is a different matter. The boy's appearance, his persistent gloom, his oracular tone, his inability ever to respond to anything as a child—all of these call attention to the fact that he is supposed to represent something. And Hardy makes the child carry more meaning than he is naturally able to. He is fate, of course, but also blighted hopes, failure, change, etc.

IRONY

The use of irony is of course commonplace in fiction, and a number of effective instances of it in Hardy's novel are to be found. In some of the instances the reader but not the character recognizes the irony; in others, both the reader and the character are aware of it. An example of the first is Jude's occupational choice of ecclesiastical stonework in medieval Gothic style in a time when medievalism in architecture is dying out or the way Arabella alienates Jude by the deception she has used to get him to marry her the first time. An example of the second is Jude's dying in Christminster, the city that has symbolized all his hopes, or the way Arabella's calling on Jude in Aldbrickham in order to reawaken his interest in her helps bring about Sue's giving herself to him.

Irony is particularly appropriate in a novel of tragic intent, in which events do not work out the way the characters expect. Certainly it is appropriate in a novel which has the kind of theme this one does. Struggling to break free of the old, the characters experience the old sufferings and failure nonetheless.

STYLE

Critics have often noted the faults in Hardy's style, and perhaps this is to be expected in a writer who was largely self-educated. Such writers can express themselves in striking and original ways, but their lack of formal education sometimes causes them to fall into awkwardness and excess. Shakespeare was, by Hardy's own admission, the greatest literary influence on him, but certainly not in the area of style. Several instances of lapses in Hardy's style might be pointed out, but one will serve to illustrate what is meant. Phillotson says to Arabella when they meet many years after she has been a student of his, "I should hardly recognize in your present portly self the slim school child no doubt you were then." It is inconceivable that anyone would talk in this way, not even the schoolmaster Phillotson. In Hardy's defense it should be said, however, that there are passages in the novel in which his style serves him quite well.

QUOTATIONS

In the novel Hardy uses a great many quotations from his reading: at the head of each part, in the narrative, and in the conversations and thoughts of the characters. Many of these are from either the Bible or Shakespeare, but they range over the whole of English literature as well. His practice here is typical of what he did in other novels. The sources of most of the quotations are given or are obvious; the others are identified in the appendices to the book by Carl Weber listed in the bibliography.

REVIEW QUESTIONS AND THEME TOPICS

1. In what specific ways are Jude and Sue counterparts? Take into account their personalities, their interests, the way they respond to things in life. (See Part Third, Chapter 3, and Phillotson's comments in Part Fourth, Chapter 4.)

2. How has Hardy contrasted Sue and Arabella? Consider what is said or shown about their appearance, manner, speech, interests, etc.

3. Compare Jude and Phillotson in their role as "husband" to Sue (Jude, of course, is never legally married to her). What do they require of her? How do they act toward her? What do they allow her to do?

4. Examine the relationship between Phillotson and Gillingham. What purpose in the novel does the latter serve in his role of friend to Phillotson? (See, for example, Part Fourth, Chapter 4, and Part Sixth, Chapter 5.)

5. Take another minor character like Anny. In relation to Arabella, what purpose does she serve in the novel? (See, for example, Part First, Chapter 9, and Part Fifth, Chapters 5, 8.)

6. Contrast the books that Jude and Sue read or have read. What do these reveal about the differences between them? (See, for example, Part First, Chapter 6, and Part Third, Chapter 4.)

7. Examine what is revealed about Sue's childhood in Marygreen. Does this help in any way to explain what Sue is as an adult? (See Part Second, Chapter 6.)

8. Look at the comments on marriage in the conversation of the characters, especially Jude and Sue. What questions about the conventions of that institution are raised? (See, for example, Part Fourth, Chapters 2-4.)

9. Examine the comments on Christminster in the conversation of the characters, especially Sue. What questions about the nature and value of that educational institution are raised? (See, for example, Part Third, Chapter 4.)

10. Look at the comments on fate made by Jude and Sue in the last part of the novel. In what way are they a questioning of conventional Christian beliefs? (See, for example, Part Sixth, Chapters 2-3.)

11. Suppose the novel were told entirely from the point of view of, say, Phillotson. In what ways would this change the nature and effect of the story?

12. For Jude the ridge-track near the Brown House outside Marygreen is a place full of significance for his life. Catalogue all the things that have happened to him here.

13. Mrs. Edlin may be thought of as a kind of local historian. List the reminiscences or anecdotes she relates in this role.

14. Study the first five paragraphs of Part Fifth, Chapter 7. This is a transitional passage summarizing the events occurring in the life of Jude and Sue for two and a half years. Is it effective? If not, explain. For example, has anything important been left out?

15. Is it a coincidence that Jude, Sue, Little Father Time, Arabella, Cartlett, Anny, and Vilbert all happen to be at the agricultural show in Stoke-Barehills at the same time? Or does the coming together of the characters grow naturally and necessarily out of the movement of the plot? (See Part Fifth, Chapter 5.)

16. It has been said that the death of the children is a sensational, melodramatic scene. What details of the scene support this contention? (See Part Sixth, Chapter 2.)

17. Take a brief scene like that in which Arabella gets Jude to make love to her. What is Hardy trying to show in this scene, and by what means does he accomplish his purpose? (See Part First, Chapter 8.)

18. Examine the scene in which Jude and Sue go on an outing during her stay at the training college in Melchester. What events, character relationships, or aspects of the characters are foreshadowed during the course of this scene? (See Part Third, Chapter 2.)

19. Is it true that Jude and Sue experience exact reversals in their beliefs? For example, at the end of the novel does Jude believe precisely what Sue did at the beginning? If not, explain. (See, for example, Part Sixth, Chapters 1, 3.)

20. To what extent do Phillotson's beliefs change during the course of the novel? If there is any change, describe it in detail. (See, for example, Part Sixth, Chapters 4-5.)

21. Hardy said that his novel was a "tragedy of unfulfilled aims." Discuss the aims that go unfulfilled, specifically among the main characters.

22. Explain the meaning of the allusion to Samson and Delilah; then, do the same for another minor symbol in the novel. (Samson and Delilah first appears in Part First, Chapter 7.)

23. Discuss the ways in which Jude's idea of Christminster affects other characters in the novel, particularly Sue and Arabella.

24. It has been said that the major symbol of Little Father Time is a failure. Document the reasons for this failure in detail. (See, for example, Part Fifth, Chapters 3-5, and Part Sixth, Chapter 2.)

25. Several instances of the use of irony which only the reader is aware of have been given; find additional examples.

26. Several instances of the use of irony which both the reader and the character are aware of have been given; find additional examples.

27. Try to justify the idea that in a tragic novel like this the use of irony is appropriate; support what you say by the use of instances of irony in the novel.

28. Find other examples, in addition to the one already given, of lapses in Hardy's style in the novel. Try to explain what is wrong with each example.

29. Find a passage in the novel in which Hardy's style is adequate to the occasion, and try to explain what is effective in his use of language.

30. Critics have said that this is the most modern of Hardy's novels. What twentieth-century novel does it seem similar to, even if only in part, and why?

SELECTED BIBLIOGRAPHY

Abercrombie, Lascelles. *Thomas Hardy: A Critical Study*. New York, 1912. An early analysis of Hardy's work as well as a summary of his attitudes.

Beach, Joseph Warren. *The Technique of Thomas Hardy*. Chicago, 1922. A study of the "structural art" of Hardy's novels, major and minor.

Guerard, Albert J. *Thomas Hardy: The Novels and Stories*. Cambridge, Mass., 1949. A study of Hardy's novels whose main purpose is "to describe the content and accomplishment of his novels in the simplest possible terms."

_____ (ed.). *Hardy: A Collection of Critical Essays*. Englewood Cliffs, N.J., 1963, Essays on Hardy's art, his major novels, his characters, and his poetry by such writers as D. H. Lawrence, John Holloway, Albert Guerard, Dorothy Van Ghent, and Samuel Hynes.

Hardy, Florence E. *The Early Life of Thomas Hardy.* London, 1928. A biography by Hardy's second wife, which was probably planned and partly written by Hardy himself.

――. *The Later Years of Thomas Hardy.* London, 1930. See Hardy, above.

Rutland, William. *Thomas Hardy: A Study of His Writings and Their Background.* Oxford, 1938. A study of the intellectual background of Hardy's thought and writing.

The Southern Review (Thomas Hardy Centennial Issue), Vol. VI (Summer 1940). Essays on various aspects of Hardy's fiction and poetry by such writers as R. P. Blackmur, F. R. Leavis, Arthur Mizener. John Crowe Ransom, and Allen Tate; those by Donald Davidson, Morton Dauwen Zabel, Delmore Schwartz, and W. H. Auden are reprinted in the collection edited by Guerard (listed above).

Weber, Carl J. *Hardy of Wessex: His Life and Literary Career.* New York, 1940. A study of Hardy's life and career, a second edition of which appeared in 1965, making use of recent scholarship and additional information from letters.

Webster, Harvey C. *On a Darkling Plain.* Chicago, 1947. A study of "the evolution of Hardy's thought and its effect upon his art."

NOTES